This book is a presentation of Weekly Reader
Books. Weekly Reader Books offers book
clubs for children from preschool through high
school. For further information write to:
WEEKLY READER BOOKS, 4343 Equity Drive,
Columbus, Ohio 43228

This edition is published by arrangement
with Checkerboard Press.

Weekly Reader is a federally registered trademark
of Field Publications.

WEEKLY READER BOOKS presents

What Is a Mountain?

A **Just Ask**™ Book

Hi, my name is Christopher!

by Chris Arvetis
and Carole Palmer

illustrated by
Terry Rose

FIELD PUBLICATIONS
MIDDLETOWN, CT.

A mountain is part of the earth that is much higher than the land around it. Mountains have long slopes and high tops.

Mountains were created a long, long time ago.
Mountains were made in several ways.
Let me show you how some were formed.

Long, long ago, movement in the earth squeezed layers of rock into folds that look like curves.

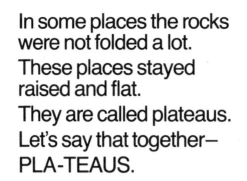

In some places the rocks were not folded a lot.
These places stayed raised and flat.
They are called plateaus.
Let's say that together—
PLA-TEAUS.

PLA-TEAUS!

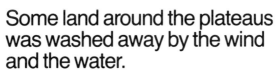

Some land around the plateaus
was washed away by the wind
and the water.
Hilly land was left.
These hills look like tabletops
and are called mesas.

A third kind of mountain
was made by volcanoes.
The hot rock from the
volcano poured out.
It made layers and layers.

A fourth kind has a round top called a dome.
The rock layers were folded upward to make domed-shaped mountains.

Plants and trees grow
on the mountain slopes.
At some high places,
it is so cold that
no plants grow.

There are many animals
in the mountains, too.
Mountain goats, sheep, deer,
moose, elk, and birds live
in the mountains.
Mountains are big and beautiful
homes for all these animals.